THE DAY I WENT TO HELL

A testimony that may help save us!

T. L. Grundy

THE DAY I WENT TO HELL
A testimony that may help save us!

TABLE OF CONTENTS

Chapter I: "Prepare For A Trip"   6

Chapter II: "How do you want it?"   8

Chapter III: "Belief is my Brand?"   14

Chapter IV: "A Road without Rage" / "Paranoia on Pavement" /

"There is no Exit"   18

Chapter V: "How does it feel?"   27

Chapter VI: True Culprit-The One Who Kayla Served   35

Chapter VII: 99.9999% Is Still Not 100   41

Chapter VIII: The Sweetness of False Hope   45

A LETTER TO THE READER   49

Acts 2:17-21

And it shall come to pass in the last days, says God; That I will pour out of

My Spirit on all flesh; Your sons and your daughters shall prophesy,

Your young men shall see visions,

Your old men shall dream dreams.

And on My menservants and My maidservants I will pour out My Spirit in those days;

And they shall prophesy.

I will show wonders in heaven above

And signs in the earth beneath:

Blood and fire and vapor of smoke.

The sun shall be turned into darkness,

And the moon into blood,

Before the coming of the great and awesome day of the Lord. And it shall come to pass

That whoever calls on the name of the Lord

Shall be saved.'

Beginning

2 Corinthians 13:5

English Standard Version

Examine yourselves to see whether you are in the faith. Test yourselves.

Or do you not realize this about yourselves, that Jesus Christ is in you? —

unless indeed you fail to meet the test!

It's not about fear but examination of self and unwavering prevailing

VICTORY!

Media&SoulProductions

here was one day that changed me. There was one day unlike any other. There was one day that everything I read concerning the biblical last days came true. And I had to go through hell to truly believe. Do you believe it? Believe it or not, I promise you this is a true and accurate account of The Day I Went To Hell.
03/14/2008

Bear with me a little longer, and I will show you that there is more to be said on God's behalf. And I get my knowledge from afar; I will ascribe justice to my Maker. Be assured that my words are not false; one perfect in knowledge is with you. God is mighty, but does not despise men; he is mighty and firm in His purpose. He does not keep the wicked alive but gives the afflicted their rights. He does not take His eyes off the righteous; He enthrones them with kings and exalts them forever. But if men are bound in chains, held fast by cords of affliction, He tells them what they have done—that they have sinned arrogantly. He makes them listen to correction and commands them to repent of their evil. If they obey and serve Him, they will spend the rest of their days in prosperity and their years in contentment. But if they do not listen, they will perish by the sword and die without knowledge.

Job: 36 1-12

I was bound in chains, held fast by cords of affliction, so God told me what I had done—that I had sinned arrogantly. I listened. I had no choice. I obey God a serve Him now with this truthful testimony: T L Grundy

Chapter I: "Prepare For A Trip"

It started better than most days. I'll say that again. The day I went to hell started better than most days. I was preparing to take a drive to pick up my daughter. On this day, everything was clicking. By that, I mean I had just gotten my haircut, and I was freshly shaved. My brand new white Nikes were on my feet. My bank account was looking pretty good. All my credit cards aligned in my wallet, seemingly just waiting patiently for use. I had rented a car for the day. It was a 2007 white Impala. I'm not that fond of the Impalas, but I was only taking a short 'three hours there and three hours back' trip. You see, I have a Jeep so usually when I take an excursion out of town that requires anything more than a one-hour drive, I'll rent a car. Hey, we all know how gas prices are, and my Jeep truly guzzles gasoline. Anyway, we won't be talking about Jeeps or gas prices; no, not in this story. Refer back to the title if you need clarity on the subject at hand.

Anyhow, I also was excited because my friend Kayla was going to go with me on this road trip. And believe me, I use the term "friend" loosely; especially in retrospect. Nevertheless, she said she would accompany me. And I was thrilled. The goal of the road trip (to my delight), was to pick up my youngest daughter, Myra. And when I had gotten her, Myra and I had plans to fly to Seattle to see my other daughter. Now then, just to keep you up to speed with the persons, places, and things of this account, let me tell you that Kayla and I were leaving Los Angeles and driving to Fresno. We were going to get Myra (my 15-year-old daughter), drive back to Los Angeles, stay the night, and fly in the morning to Seattle, WA. Got it? I don't think you do. I mean, you're probably with me story-wise, but we all know that we make plans, but God determines the steps. And He determined mine in a major way. And my steps came in a matter of miles and miles and miles on an eternal road to nowhere.

Chapter II: "How do you want it?"

Once Kayla and I were on the road, we put some Tupac (of which I always keep a great supply) in the CD player. We had some small conversations paired with even less eye contact. I was driving, so I had to keep my eyes on the road. We stopped to eat at Kayla's favorite Mexican restaurant. All the while petting and tenderly playing with each other. She ordered the Fajitas. They were served with grilled meat strips, stripped peppers, and onions on a corn tortilla. I had Enchiladas with chicken, cheese, beans, potatoes, and vegetables. And then we were set for dessert consisting of deep-fried dough, coated in cinnamon sugar and dipped in caramel. They were sweet on the outside, fluffy and moist on the inside, and also very delicious.

Once we had eaten, we were off on our way to Fresno. So there I was, on the N 405 freeway, with my sexy friend Kayla next to me. Kayla, I would describe her as quick-witted and captivating. She is a delightful person; you can't take your eyes off her. Her style, I would describe her as sultry because she has an old soul, but she is only in her late 20s. Her voice is raspy. Her skin is bronze, with charming freckles around her nose. Her smile is rich and humorous. Her hair is straightened and surrounds her face in a manner reminiscent of statues depicting Cleopatra. She has vibrant green eyes. Her nature, obliging. During conversations, her favorite phrase is, "Please, tell me more." I think that's one of the main reasons why I like her so much. She is very unassuming and non-judgemental. She has one of those Care free spirits that help to relax the people she is around.

We are now playing and bumping Tupac's "How Do You Want It" (at the highest level). We were both dancing in our seats and laughing loudly while harmonizing the chorus, "How do you want it? How does it feel? Comin' up as a brotha in the cash game Livin' in the fast lane, ah, for real… How do you want it? (Yeah) How do you feel? Comin' up as a brotha in the cash game Livin' in the fast lane, ah, for real…

"How do you want it? How does it feel? Comin' up as a brotha in the cash game Livin' in the fast lane, ah, for real… How do you want it? (Yeah) How do you feel? Comin' up as a brotha in the cash game Livin' in the fast lane, ah, for real…

I was well-groomed, and my outfit was fresh. At the start of the year, I had made a New Year's resolution that I would stay in the weight room. I had kept my resolution. For the last 6 months, I have been working out three times a week. And my muscles were happily enjoying the development of those workouts. My body was hard and ripped. I had a pocket full of cash and a wallet full of gold and platinum credit cards; which included Triple-A Auto Club, just in case we had any problems. You see, in my mind, I was prepared for the worst.

I was eating up the highway in my rented, all-white Chevy Impala. And I was super stoked that I was only three hours away from picking up my beloved youngest daughter. I was feeling high. I was feeling good. I was untouchable. How Do You Want? How does it feel…? It was still blaring from the CD player. What could go wrong? And then he attacked! I felt a foreign presence. The atmosphere changed abruptly. It was as if I felt a heaviness that wasn't there a second ago. It was a perception of being crowded. It was a change or a "changeling," as best as I can explain it. Something was different; a shift of sorts.

It was the type of feeling you have when somebody comes to your social gathering, party, event, or even to your home uninvited. It was as if someone had the self-willed audacity to invite themselves, but not even courteously. They are rude, obnoxious, and entitled. The unwelcomed have taken over your home.

At first, it was subtle. It was weird. I wasn't particularly alarmed. But what alarmed me or concerned me was that Kayla had fallen silent— deathly silent. I mean, the music was very loud, and the baseline was incredibly intense—but I could feel a stillness or hush.

I could only see Kayla from my peripheral vision. And I could have sworn she was staring at me with her face inches from mine. For some reason, it looked as if Kayla was scrutinizing me. It's weird, but I felt she was trying to figure out who I was. It also somewhat seemed as if Kayla was gone, and a stranger rode with me. I felt sure I was riding with an unfamiliar person. And from my side vision, I could still see her staring at me; intently. Closely. I felt she was waiting for me to turn and look at her. Something said, "Don't look at her," and again, it said, "Don't look at her." This was not a voice outside my head. This was not a voice in my head. It was just some type of inkling. You see, I have daughters, and sometimes we play this type of game where they will stare at me real intently from the side, and as soon as I turn to look at them, they pretend they weren't looking at me; we do it four or five times, then I'll catch them (if I'm real quick) staring at me and making these crazy faces, and we'll laugh. It's just something dad and kids have picked up over the years. It's fun. It's goofy. But Kayla had been watching me carefully. And I had only kept my eyes forward. A few minutes had gone by, and I realized that Kayla's eyes were not on me anymore. That's when I felt that deathly silence. I had to finally look over at Kayla. I was compelled to. I knew something was not right. I felt I wanted to do anything in the world besides looking over at the person who was next to me. But I had to, and I did.

 When I turned to look at Kayla, all I could do to describe how she looked was in a trance. And I don't mean that she was staring into space or looking dreamingly. No. I mean, her fists were balled up tightly. They were like vice grips. Kayla is a fair-skinned person. I could see the blood in her hands at a standstill, and her knuckles had turned white due to the extreme pressure. I looked further and saw that her arms were being held against her sides. She was stiff, straight, and petrified as a board. I saw that her lips were curled up inside of her mouth so far that it appeared they reached down her throat. And her mouth gave the impression that it was gone. Her nose was drawn low and so unnatural that it sat in the area where her mouth should have. Her eyes were battened down tight and unyielding. This was the same person I had known for about five years, but because she was so wounded and scrunched up so tightly, her face looked like something else. The figure that sat next to me didn't look human. Her body had seemingly transformed. I immediately turned the CD player off.

How Do You….Click. Once the music stopped immediately, I could hear Kayla in an eerie labored hum, chant, or a loud mum. I tried, but if truth be told, I couldn't decipher what the sound was. Her lips were not moving. She made this sound through her nose and throat. The sound Kayla was making went like, "ahhhhhhhhhh mmmmmmmmmmmmmmm!" It was a constant tone. It was blood-curdling. To this day, I have never heard of any type of sound like it. It was a sound accompanied by a look of extreme pain, terror, and panic. It looked like Kayla was in the ultimate fight; the fight for her life.

 I at first thought that Kayla was playing. I thought she was trying to trick me. But that thought never was sincere; just wishful thinking. I hoped she was joking with me. I had hoped she was trying to trick me. The next thought was more substantial. I thought to myself, "Kayla is having a seizure. And she may very well swallow her tongue and die." I immediately started looking for the nearest exit so I could get her some help. I was scared.

I was scared because I truly had feelings for this woman. And scared because I felt I was probably the cause of her going into this convulsion. Kayla stayed that way while I pretended to be calm. But I was drastically looking for the nearest exit. But no exit was coming up. So I finally tried to comfort her. I said, "Kayla, I love you, and I'm with you. You are ok. I'm going to pull over at the nearest exit, and I'm going to get you some help. Just hold on Kayla!" All the while, I was praying that God would help and allow an exit to come up. And Kayla kept making that strange and frightening uhhhhhhmmmmmmmmmmmmmnnnnnuuummm sound! And her face and body stayed wound up as tightly as a drum. And still stiff. And because of the pressure keeping her lips curled in her mouth, Kayla's veins in her face were starting to materialize. All of her femininity was gone. She looked like a man. I hardly recognized her. I began to panic. I was so concerned about her life. I thought she was dying. *Not everyone that saith unto me, Lord, Lord, shall enter into the kingdom of heaven; but he that doeth the will of my Father which is in heaven. Many will say to me on that day, Lord, Lord, have we not prophesied in thy name? And in thy name have cast out devils? And in thy name done many wonderful works? And then will I profess unto them, I never knew you: depart from me, ye that work iniquity. Therefore whosoever heareth these sayings of mine, and doeth them, I will liken him unto a wise man, which built his house upon a rock: And the rain descended, and the floods came, and the winds blew, and beat upon that house; and it fell not: for it was founded upon a rock.*

Matthew 7 21-23

Chapter III: "Belief is my Brand?"

Well reader, this is the part of the account where I need you to stay with me. Please try to keep your mind clear and open so you can understand the things that are about to unfold. And remember, this account is accurate and truthful. This happened on Friday, March 14th. I'm writing this account on Sunday, March 16th. And yes reader, this is scary. I'm getting scared writing it. But I have to write it so you may believe and get closer to God, or start believing in him altogether. I had to write this so soon after it happened because it is so important that I get everything right; every seemingly little detail needs to be accurate. It is critical that you, the reader, believe. I have to make you believe. It is the only way that I truly will believe I'm ok. I know that "he" or the "uninvited" in his evil would never allow me to help save people. Helping people goes against "his" beliefs, so if I can get you to believe and/or change one thing about your life; I'm ok. And if I can just prevent one person (hopefully multitudes) from being lost, then I must be ok. But until you believe and change or get saved, I'm unsure if I'm still here. Please stay open and continue to follow this account:

At this point, I started driving fast, still looking for any place to get off the freeway. I looked up and read that an exit was coming up, so I started moving over to the right lane while looking back over my shoulder to make sure of a clear and safe lane change. But while I was searching and maneuvering the car, I realized that Kayla had stopped having her so-called seizure. I'm not sure how long it lasted (mainly because I wasn't sure when it started; remember I had been, for some reason, frightened to look over at her for about 10 -15 minutes), but if I had to estimate, I would say it went on for about 20 long, frightful minutes.

And now, when I looked at Kayla, she looked calm. She looked peaceful. She looked confident. And she looked back at me. The expression on her face was tender. It was the face a loving and nurturing mom would give to her child. It was warm. And when she spoke to me, she spoke with sincerity, confidence, resolve, seduction, and power. She tenderly put her hand on my chin and turned my face so that my face and her face were inches apart, she looked me square in the eyes, and she said flatly, "Terry, we are dead." I said, "Huh?" She said, "We died, and we're in hell." Again, I asked, "Huh, what did you say, Kayla?" And she repeated herself. But this time, her voice cut through the calmness, and spittle flew from her mouth, as she shrieked from the top of her lungs, "WE ARE DEAD! AND–WE–ARE–IN–HELLLLLLLLLLLLL!" She dragged out the word hell. It's not like I hadn't heard her the first time. But when a person asks, "Huh, what

did you say?" nine out of 10, you're just wanting them to say, "Nothing,"
or "Never mind." Also, we say "huh," because we want more clarity. She
seemed to understand that and gave it to me. She said again, "We died, and
we're in hell. We are never leaving. WE ARE DEAD!"
While she is speaking, I am getting cold. Her odorless, cold breath is giving me a cold sweat. I'm shivering in southern California. And my heart
is beating itself out of my chest. I can hear the beats of my heart clogging
my ears. Her declarations came out of nowhere. And now I'm sweating
profusely. I was pale and colorless. It was a feeling of absolute terror when
she was screeching that she and I were dead. I thought to myself that I
was not just merely going to get off the freeway and get her help, but I
was going to get off the freeway and take Miss Kayla home. I thought to
myself that this woman cannot handle this trip. She needed to go home
until she got over the delusion she was experiencing. You see, I wanted to
help her. I also told myself that the whole thing regarding what she was
saying was sort of humorous. Scary, yes, but humorous as well. I worked
at convincing myself it was cute in a childlike way. I told myself not to be
scared, especially now that she had come out of her seizure. Now I think
I'll take a second and tell you (since I've had some time to think about it)
she was not having a seizure. I believe she was in a sort of trance, spell,
or possession (In my opinion. You are free to make your conclusion). I
believe she was receiving orders. Orders on what to do from a person she
called "him," or "he." But we'll talk about that in a short while. I was
relieved that Kayla had loosened her body and opened her eyes. She also
seemed resolved. But I still was concerned. I mean, not too many people
go around talking about how they're dead, and they're in hell; and that I'm
with them! Also, what concerned me was that Kayla would one second
appear calm and resolved toward her feelings about being dead and in hell,

and then one minute later, she would seem hysterical. Then, she would begin to shout that she was dead and in hell, in a frightful fit of realization. *Now the Spirit speaketh expressly, that in the latter times some shall depart from the faith, giving heed to seducing spirits, and doctrines of devils; Speaking lies in hypocrisy; having their conscience seared with a hot iron;* **1 Timothy 4 1-2**

You see since Kayla repeatedly said we are dead and in hell over and over again and trying to figure out what happened to me (us), I have done some extensive digging in these last couple of days. And through research and fact-finding, I have learned that repetition makes any message stronger. It's called the illusory truth effect: humans believe some information to be correct after repeated and repeated exposure. We rate repeated statements as more truthful than non-repeated ones. Repetition creates the comfort of familiarity. When our brains find something easier to process, we like it more than a similar thing that is not as easily processed. So the more you repeat your brand or tagline, the more likable it will become.

**Chapter IV: "A Road without Rage" / "Paranoia on Pavement" /
"There is no Exit"**

I continued to stay calm and drive. I located the exit. I got off the
freeway. I had been traveling northbound on the 405. I immediately got
back on the freeway and started heading back the way we had come;
southbound on the freeway taking her home. We were now again on the
freeway. I looked over to Kayla, and I said in the most reassuring voice I
could find, "Kayla, I'm taking you home." I also told her not to worry; that
it was cool. I told her I would just take her home, and then I'll turn around
and get back on the road. No problem. I'm not upset. I understand that
sometimes we have crazy feelings. By her expression, it looked like my
attempt to comfort her was not working. The expression on her face made
me think she was completely scared. And not just scared, her appearance

looked like she was terrified.

And the Spirit of God came upon Azariah the son of Oded: And he went out to meet Asa, and said unto him, Hear ye me, Asa, and all Judah and Benjamin; The Lord is with you, while ye be with him; and if ye seek him, he will be found of you; but if ye forsake him, he will forsake you.

Chronicles 15:2

I knew she was scared because she started praying in a loud voice. Her prayers were screams. She prayed to overcome me. She prayed to defeat me. She prayed for strength and clarity. But even though I consider myself a Christian; and I love prayer, and I love people who pray, I felt continuously uneasy by Kayla's prayers. I finally realized why, and I turned to Kayla and asked her, "Whom are you praying to?" She stopped praying, and she said calmly, "Terry, why don't you get it?" And she turned her eyes to the freeway and started reading the exits. She read each exit sign we passed in a firm and commanding voice. And each time she read a few signs, she would turn to me and say," Don't you finally get it?" And then it hit me. Realization chilled me like an icy winter's wind. At the same time, I got the realization she screamed, "All the exits are the same! We died! We are in hell! Our punishment is to spend eternity on this freeway!" And then she turned and once again started reading each exit sign we passed. And once again though I had sped up, each exit was the same as the one she had already read. She then turned to me and asked me point-blank, why I turned my back on God. She asked me why I chose her over God. She said, "Terry, we are dead and in hell." She said that she died on this freeway years ago. And she keeps going back to get people like me. But it was my choice. She said I chose this. And now I was dead.

For the eyes of the Lord run to and fro throughout the whole earth, to shew himself strong in the behalf of them whose heart is perfect toward

2 Chronicles 16:9

I'll tell you, reader, now I'm beyond concerned. I'm flat-out scared. I continued. I continued to drive, and now I'm speeding and passing cars. I'm flying on the freeway. I am weaving in and out of traffic. Moving between car after car. I'm reaching speeds of 90 to 100 miles an hour. I am frantically driving. The cars I passed seemed to pay me no attention. The cars I passed all seemed to be going at the exact speed with the same amount of space between each car. No one was honking the horn at me, even though I am weaving in and out of traffic. I'm passing cars on the left side, and I'm passing cars on the right side. No one even glanced at me or even gave me a second look. I see no law enforcement. No one has road rage. In front of me is just a road and cut-and-paste images of other cars. The sun in the sky is in the same place as it started. I'm driving, looking for something different to happen. I'm driving, trying to get to any other destination. And though Kayla was not smiling, I could tell the situation was not so dire, it would probably humor her by my stubbornness not to understand that I was dead. But it's truly not funny to her. She is not happy. Her attitude is like, "What a strange thing that you don't get the picture." She wants me to understand where I'm at and why I'm here. And the answer according to her is "in hell," and the reason is because "I chose her over God." And Moses made haste, and bowed his head toward the earth, and worshipped. And he said, If now I have found grace in thy sight, O Lord, let my Lord, I pray thee, go among us; for it is a stiffnecked people; and pardon our iniquity and our sin, and take us for thine inheritance. And he said, Behold, I make a covenant: before all thy people I will do marvels, such as have not been done in all the earth, nor in any nation: and all the people among which thou art shall see the work of the Lord: for it is a terrible thing that I will do with thee. Observe thou that which I command thee this day: behold, I drive out before thee the Amorite, and the Canaanite, and the Hittite, and the Perizzite, and the Hivite, and the Jebusite. Take heed to thyself, lest thou make a covenant with the inhabitants of the land whither thou goest, lest it be for a snare in the midst of thee: But ye shall destroy their altars, break their images, and cut down their groves: For thou shalt worship no other god: for the Lord, whose name is Jealous, is a jealous God: Lest thou make a covenant with the inhabitants of the land, and they go a whoring after their gods, and do sacrifice unto their gods, and one call thee, and thou eat of his sacrifice, And thou take of their daughters unto thy sons, and their daughters go a whoring after their gods, and make thy sons go a whoring after their gods. Thou shalt make thee no molten gods.

Exodus 34: 8-17

I finally had to pull over. I had to take a break; a break from driving but mostly a break from Kayla. I had to think, and what I didn't mention earlier was that even though the exit signs stayed the same, there was no exit ramp, none, nada, zippo, naught. I could not exit off the freeway. So instead, I pulled to the side of the freeway on a piece of dirt road. It was 12:30 in the afternoon, on Friday. It was too early in the day for traffic jams and cars, 'zoomed' along the freeway at normal speeds. The sky was bright. It was a warm mid-day. We had been on the road for about 45 minutes. Kayla made it very clear we were not to stop driving. She said we must continue driving. She said we are dead. We are in hell. Our hell is to spend eternity on this freeway. I got out of the car. When I got out of the car, I heard the cars zooming by. And I heard Kayla say again we are dead. Still trying to convince me we were dead, she said, "Look at all the drivers in those cars. They are the same cars that keep passing over and over. She yelled, "Take a look!" I did. And short of my mind being vacant, I was looking at the same cars and the same faces that were driving those cars. I see the same guy hauling lumber that I saw while I was trying to get off the freeway. And it wasn't many different faces, but it was two or three of the same faces in many different cars. Every driver is sitting straight up and looking straight forward. I mean, whoever set this up was either dumb thinking this would trick me, or genuinely wanted me to understand and realize what an idiot I was and that I had been driving around on the same patch of the freeway for 45 minutes; seeing the same two or three faces in a few different cars. It was a stage. And not a very convincing stage; low budget and basic. It was 'cut and paste.' Now, I'm over and done with just being scared. I'm petrified. I'm shocked and colorless. I'm standing still, but I'm frantic. My heart is racing, but with nowhere to put my energy. I'm a fight-or-flight. And there is no one to fight, and there is no place for flight. I hear Kayla say, "Don't you see we are dead? We died. We are in hell, and our punishment is to drive on this freeway. Forever." I got back in the car. I turned to Kayla, still trying to make sense of what was going on. I asked, "When did you know?" She then told me some of her check-ered stories. She said she died on this freeway years ago. She said she lost her soul, and she keeps going back to get others. She said I chose her. She said I made the decision. She asked me why [I chose her over God] but didn't wait for the answer. She continued and told me that she does her duty for him now. And since I'm dead and I'm in hell, and now, I must do his duty too. She said, "Come on, let's go!" Ok, I said, "But first Kayla, let me ask you some more questions."

Well, reader, let me interject right here to take a second to tell you a little about me; and an even smaller amount about Kayla. I think it's important

for you to realize who you're dealing with. I consider myself a sane, ratio-
nal, investigative person, who does not jump to unsubstantial conclusions.
I gather facts. I make logical deductions. Furthermore, I'm not a kid. I
have 'been there and done that,' if you will. I don't even drink alcohol. I'm
GOD fearing etc. I'm telling you this because remember, I need you to believe. Therefore I have to do my best to tell you as accurately as possible
who I am and exactly what I experienced that day.

A double-minded man is unstable in all his ways.

 James 1:8

*Draw near to God, and He will draw near to you. Cleanse your hands,
you sinners; and purify your hearts, you double-minded.*

James 4:8

*I hate those who are double-minded, But I love Your law. You are my hid-
ing place and my shield; I wait for Your word. Depart from me, evildoers,
That I may observe the commandments of my God.*

Psalm 119:113-115

In addition, reader, I know the scriptures well. I was baptized in January
1996. I dedicated my life to GOD then, and I have been studying the Bible
intently for years. I know that the Bible says that when Jesus comes back,
he's going to come like a thief in the night (1 Thessalonians 5:2). I know
that the Bible says that Jesus died for my sins, and whoever believes in
him will be saved. I know that the scriptures say that when Jesus comes
back, he will judge the world, and for those whose names are not found in
the Book of Life, there will be no hope for them. I know all these things,
and Kayla knows them too. *We have faith and believe in one God. See, one
thing you must understand is that the Bible says, "You say you have faith
for you believe that there is one God. Good for you! Even the demons believe this, and they tremble in Terror." James 2:19.* And Kayla and I used

to go to the same church I was presently a member. She had previously
been going for years. Something had happened that hurt her faith. She fell
away from the body and eventually fell away from GOD. I was presently
on the same road as Kayla, literally and figuratively. I had stopped sub-
mitting to the culture of the church. I was upset at the head evangelist at
my church. I became open with him about Kayla and me, and he, in my
opinion, handled it wrong. His intentions were good. His method was not.
I don't blame him. I take full responsibility.

*For if we sin wilfully after that, we have received the knowledge of the
truth, there remaineth no more sacrifice for sins, But a certain fearful
looking for of judgment and fiery indignation, which shall devour the
adversaries. He that despised Moses' law died without mercy under two
or three witnesses: Of how much sorer punishment, suppose ye, shall he
be thought worthy, who hath trodden under foot the Son of God, and hath
counted the blood of the covenant, wherewith he was sanctified, an unholy
thing, and hath done despite unto the Spirit of grace? For we know him
that hath said, Vengeance belongeth unto me, I will recompense, saith the
Lord. And again, The Lord shall judge his people. It is a fearful thing to
fall into the hands of the living God.*

Hebrews 10:26-31

The bottom line, I was disconnected from the body. I had stopped being a
part of my church for about three months. I and Kayla had started spending a lot of time together. In my heart, I was done with going to church.
Physically, I had not been going to church. Spiritually I was deficient. I
just had yet to tell myself. You see, I had made the decision, but I didn't
know I had made it.

You see, we've all seen lions attack their prey. At first, the lion hides and
stalks the prey. Then, they attack the group by some type of diversion.

And when the prey gets spooked by the lions, they all run– but they all run together, and they remain safe from the predators. But as soon as one of the prey runs off by themselves, they are vulnerable to attack, and possibly death. The lions want to feed off the weak. The lion is constantly looking for the weak. The lion is constantly looking for the prey that has run away from the protection of the herd. This is the same way Satan attacks us and tries to scare us into leaving the protection of our friends and loved ones. Kayla and I were two souls alone. We were ripe for slaughter. And we were at this point surrounded by salivating hunger-crazed predators. I could feel them, and Kayla could see them. I was fighting to try and fight them off, but there were too many of them, and I had no armor and no weapon. I was alone.

One more point I'm compelled to make before I continue with this account is to tell you that I had befriended the enemy, and he had turned on me. I had chosen the pleasures of the flesh. Honestly, I know I had many opportunities to repent from my sins. But I felt like a lot of Christians do. I felt everything was cool. I thought that I'd be able to jump off the ship when it starts burning. I'll escape in the nick of time. The way I was feeling reminds me of my perspective when I was six, and couldn't understand how people died in airplane crashes. If an airplane was about to crash, I usually wonder why a person won't just jump out of the airplane seconds before it hits the ground; and thus save themselves. It sounds pretty childish, right? Well, that's how I had been living my life. I had been waiting to jump out of the crashing plane.

But one thing I didn't factor in was gravity. I was a grown man living my life with no rules, structure, or boundaries. I was living in any way that suited me. And justifying it and reasoning like a six-year-old child.

Let whoever has ears hear and whoever has eyes see...

Matthew 11:15

Therefore now amend your ways and your doings, and obey the voice of the Lord your God, and the Lord will repent him of the evil that he hath pronounced against you.

Jerimiah 26:13

And he said unto them, He that hath ears to hear, let him hear.

Mark 4:9

Chapter V: "How does it feel?"

I turned to Kayla and asked her when she realized we were dead and in hell. I asked her how we died. She kept saying that it did not matter. "What does it matter, Terry? You and I are in hell. We turned our backs on God." But she also again confessed, "I died on this freeway years ago." She said she died in a car accident, and her soul was lost. And she has to stay driving on this freeway forever. I could see the sincerity in what she was saying. So I tried to rationalize. I tried to convince her about the Father (GOD) and His unending mercy. I told her that God would forgive her. I pleaded, "GOD would forgive us!" I told her all we had to do was pray. She looked at me again with compassion and said, "Terry, It's too

late! You died. You chose me over God. God has abandoned you because
of your choice. And now it's too late for his mercy. It's too late for me.
And it's too late for you! Come on, let's drive! This is our hell!"
I screamed, "No!" I said, "We're leaving. We're going home." I put the
car in drive (I had never turned the engine off). I remember the car skid-
ding back onto traffic and the Highway. I was determined to prove her
wrong. Once I started driving again, Kayla watched me intently. And I
watched her from my peripheral vision while keeping most of my focus on
the road. I watched the cars around me. I watched my gas hand to see if it
moved. I watched for the police because I was seriously speeding. I wasn't
concerned about a ticket. I longed for a ticket or to get pulled over. I saw
no police officers. And Kayla still watched me with compassion and moth-
erly concern. And as soon as the first exit sign came up, she began once
again to read the words; out loud. And believe it or not, it was once again
the same signs we had seen over and over before. I was distraught. I kept
driving. But each exit we passed did not yield an exit ramp. And Kayla
would not stop reading those signs!
I thought to myself that it must be her hell to continue to read the signs,
and my hell was to continue to drive. We were linked in life by our sins,
and it seems we were also linked in hell. I was praying and asking GOD
not to abandon me. And when I prayed, Kayla would just look at me and
say, "It's too late. It's too late. It's too late. You died. We are in Hell." I
want you to know that Kayla was just as terrified as I was. But the only
difference was that Kayla knew we were dead, and I had yet to give in
to it 100%. Kayla wanted me to open my eyes and realize where I was.
And she wanted me to realize there was no hope. And she wanted me to
realize why. And she kept talking convincingly as I continued to drive
on the same patch of freeway, seeing the same exits. As she kept talking

repeatedly as I kept seeing the same faces in many different cars, I started to believe. She knew I was starting to understand, and she gave me more instructions. Kayla again said that she had died on this freeway years ago. She said that she was in hell, and now she serves him. She also told me that I would have to serve him now; and forever. She said she goes back just to win people for him. She said I had to do the same. I had no choice. She said I chose her, and that's why I'm in Hell. She said there is no going back. We are in hell together. The way Kayla was talking was like we were a team. And her job was to fill me in on the facts. Her job was not to comfort me but to get me resolved. Resolved that I had died and went to hell; resolved that I had chosen her over God; resolved that I could never leave; and resolved that I was now his and I will do his bidding. At this point, I am horrified. I am distraught. I am sorry. I'm in the car with Kayla. My mind is racing a hundred miles an hour. But like the car, going nowhere. Kayla is filled with nothing less than extreme terror. And she is continually reading the same exit signs. Again, reader, I was at the point where I was starting to believe. I started feeling hopeless. I started to feel even less scared. I'm beginning to lay into it. But I am still fighting. So what do I do? I finally pulled the car over once again. And Kayla shrieks, "We are dead! We are in hell! We need to keep driving on this patch of freeway forever! Terry, keep driving!" I stop the car but keep the car running, and I get out of it once again. I leave the driver's door open. I start screaming again. I scream, "No God! Please, no, GOD! I couldn't have missed you! I was so close! I couldn't have missed it! Please forgive me. I'm sorry!"

But I have this against you, that you tolerate that woman Jezebel, who calls herself a prophetess and is teaching and seducing my servants to practice sexual immorality and to eat food sacrificed to idols. I gave her time to repent, but she refuses to repent of her sexual immorality. Behold,

I will throw her onto a sickbed, and those who commit adultery with her I will throw into great tribulation unless they repent of her works, and I will strike her children dead. And all the churches will know that I am he who searches mind and heart, and I will give to each of you according to your works.

Revelation 2:20-23

Be sober-minded; be watchful. Your adversary the devil, prowls around like a roaring lion, seeking someone to devour. Resist him, firm in your faith, knowing that the same kinds of suffering are being experienced by your brotherhood throughout the world.

1Peter 5:8-9

O foolish Galatians! Who has bewitched you? It was before your eyes that Jesus Christ was publicly portrayed as crucified.

Galatians 3:1

Finally, be strong in the Lord and the strength of his might. Put on the whole armor of God, that you may be able to stand against the schemes of the devil. For we do not wrestle against flesh and blood, but the rulers, against the authorities, against the cosmic powers over this present darkness, against the spiritual forces of evil in the heavenly places. Therefore take up the whole armor of God, that you may be able to withstand in the evil day, and having done all, to stand firm. Stand therefore, having fastened on the belt of truth, and having put on the breastplate of righteousness ...

Ephesians 6:10-18

Kayla is watching me. Her voice is shrill, "It's too late. Just keep driving." The freeway is loud. I hear the cars flying by. Kayla is 15 feet away from me. But I can hear her clearly as if she were still standing right next to me. Like someone had a state-of-the-art sound system that canceled out and separated all background noise. If it wasn't for the fact that I was scared, crying, and possibly dead, I would have thought it cool. I can hear her yelling, "Terry, we are dead." She is yelling so loud and forcibly that I can even see the veins in her neck pulsating while screaming and pronouncing every syllable, "T-E-R-R-Y WE ARE DEAD. DEAD. DEAD." She went back and forth from, "Terry, we are dead" to simply just saying the word "dead dead dead dead.dead.dead.dead.dead.dead." I mean, reader, I've never been a violent or impatient person. But I can wholeheartedly tell you that I truly wanted to kill her so she would just shut up. I likened her to a kindergartener saying, "Nah Nah Na Nah Nah Nah Nah Na Nah Na" while bullying their schoolmates. I yelled in my head, "Stop! Stop! Stop!" How ironic that she just wouldn't stop telling me we are dead, and I was so frustrated by her telling me that I wanted it to make her dead. I think I honestly can say that we go our whole lives from newborn to maybe 80-100 years old, and no one ever says these three words to us: "You Are Dead."

You may hear, "You are going to die." You may hear, "You almost died." You may hear, "I'm going to kill you." You may hear, "I hope you don't die." You may hear, "A loved one died." You may also be playing a video game, and someone says, "You are dead." I get that, but they're not talking about you, they're talking about your avatar. Also, I've been playing basketball at a park, and one player gets fouled hard by another player, and he will turn to the person that's guarding him, and he'll say, "If you purposely foul me one more time, "you're dead!" I've been at a nightclub and seen patrons get so angry with other people (for various reasons) they have told them, "You're dead!" But those are examples of threats. Those are not declarations. Kayla was not threatening me, she was giving me a declaration. A declaration of death. But we go our whole lives, and there is

0% chance that we will ever hear those three words declared to us. And I heard those words over and over again. My mind, my spirit, and my very soul were grieving. Those three words were killing me. I think that question could be a winner for the game show, Jeopardy. Name a combination of words you will never hear in your lifetime. ''I know, 'You -Are -Dead!' Yes, that is the correct answer.

 I can see her eyes narrow and her arms gesturing like she's trying her best to get me to take it in. "Terry, we are dead." She is a robot repeating it over and over. You would think with the loud freeway and the multitude of cars passing by that, I wouldn't be able to hear her. But it was weird. It was like it was her and me alone amongst all the cars and all the noise. She and I were isolated in a vacuum. She and I are together in the life of sin, and now she and I, in the punishment in death. She and I are the only two here in this particular hell. Two people who used one another while alive. Two people who now despised and hated each other in this hell. Joined were we. Complicit in our sinful work to get to where we are now. My Crimey. And now, together, we are in the same cell. We are in that same prison. And now we were together walking the yard, joined in eternal punishment. I felt sick. I felt closed in. And it seemed as if we were the only people – her and I in this world. Or this hell, according to her. No car stops to help. No car even seems to care what we're doing. I start tearing my clothes. I ripped my sweatshirt off. I ripped off my shoes. I pulled at my face. I screamed out. But nothing changed. I cried, "God no. Did I miss it? God no; I was so close." I turned back to the car and Kayla. I needed answers. I asked, "Kayla, tell me. Tell me, when did I die? How did I die? What happened? Did I get in a car accident? Was I shot?" She didn't answer. Immediately my mind tried to trace back all my activities that day. I thought back to when I was waiting to get my haircut at this barbershop in Compton. Two guys were in the shop talking about their friend who had gotten killed the previous night. I remembered this unscrupulous guy coming into the shop. I wondered if he started shooting in the barbershop and he accidentally or purposely killed me. I started thinking about when Kayla and I smoked half a blunt while driving on the freeway. I remembered being close to one of the cars and wondered if I crashed and died. Darling reader, let me just tell you, my mind was all over the place. I don't know why, but I started thinking about the movie Ghost I saw years ago starring Demi Moore and Patrick Swayze. It's a pretty popular movie. You probably know the gist of it. If you don't, it's about someone that died, and they cannot leave until they solve the riddle of their murder and let their beloved partner know she is in danger too. But that plot is not what I'm thinking about. I am thinking about the subplot about a medium played by Whoopi Goldberg, and what she does is that she helps the dead understand they are dead and helps them to move on to another realm. If I died, did I not know I was dead? Do I need somebody (maybe Kayla) to help me realize I'm dead? Because one thing I do know about death is that it is the great unknown.

I screamed at Kayla to please tell me when I died. I screamed to Kayla to tell me how I died. She didn't answer. But she reaffirmed that we had died. We were in hell. We were never going to leave. And I should get in the car and DRIVE! Well, those types of questions were getting me nowhere, so I asked other questions. I said, "Ok if we are dead, do you feel this?" and I grabbed her arm. She paused, looked at my hand on her arm, and she sighed, "Yes, I feel," still looking at my hand on her. Kayla said very sarcastically, "Yes, in hell, we can still feel." She looked at me menacingly and said, "Don't you feeeeeel?" She stretched out the word feel. And after she asked that question, she just peered at me. Peering is what she did because her gaze was piercing. As she gazed at me piercingly, her question lingered in the air. The question she asked answered itself as she gazed at me. She looked through me. She looked inside me. She looked at me and waited, seemingly wanting my answer, but my mouth did not answer. But my mind, my spirit, and my body screamed: "Yes!" My mouth remained loyal and defiant. The pink tornado in my mouth held still. But again, my body, my mind, and my spirit betrayed me, and it answered for my mouth; and said over and over: "Yes! Yes, I feel! Yes, I feel! Yes!" My thoughts confessed that I do feel—with all my spirit, body, and mind. And she said it again. She reiterated it. It came again lest I forgot. She said it anew:" We-are-dead. We-are-in-hell."

 I just looked back at her because yes, I did feel something. I felt regret, pain, sorrow, loneliness, stupidity, and the like. Yes, I could still feel something. I asked her if we could drink or eat. Again she gave the same answer, "Terry, we are in hell." I said to myself, "Ok, I know the scriptures. I know the Bible says if you're not ready when Jesus comes back, there will be just weeping and gnashing of teeth," (both of which I was presently doing). In that place, there will be weeping and gnashing of teeth, when you see Abraham and Isaac and Jacob and all the prophets in the kingdom of God, but you cast out.

Luke 13:28

The master of that servant will come on a day when he does not expect him, and at an hour he does not know and will cut him in pieces and put him with the hypocrites. In that place, there will be weeping and gnashing of teeth.

Matthew 24:50-51

Chapter VI: True Culprit-The One Who Kayla Served

S... So I just thought I would ask Kayla another hypothetical question. I asked her point-blank, "Can we have sex?" (But I didn't use that nice word. I used the epithet. I used the f-word. I want to keep this rated G for the general audience, so let's just say the "f word is an epithet word, ok?) I will never forget the look she gave me. Never! She gave me this look that said this was the dumbest question I had asked her today. No, this was the dumbest question anybody had asked in the history of hell and heaven; period. And she said exactly what I was thinking. She asked, ``Can we 'epithet word?'" She sarcastically snorted, "We have 'epithet word' we 'epithet word' all the time. We 'epithet word' like crazy!" She sarcastically mimicked me and asked again, "Can we 'epithet word?' Oh Terry," she chided, "We have 'epithet word'! "And that's why we're here!" Her eyes said, "You idiot!"

Yes, it was true. We had. I knew it just like her. She knew I knew it too. I was asking the dumbest question in the history of time. Please, reader, I want to continue with this account, but please allow me to expand on this point first. You see, the question I asked Kayla was equivalent to Adam asking Eve (after eating the apple and discovering the difference between good and evil), "If by any chance he could still eat apples from that tree?" Adam may ask that question, but I can tell you with 100% certainty that he would not even for one second want to touch or go near those apples. The lure of the tree was gone; the excitement and the adventure of the tree were no more. Those apples were the lie that caused "the fall of man," and do you think for one second he wants to eat one after finding the truth? (Note: I do realize the fruit was not necessarily an apple. The Bible just says it was forbidden fruit, for all you Bible scholars.)

It was the same with me. I had just lost my soul for all eternity. The last thing I ever wanted to do was reenact the thing I did to lose it. Not today; and not in a million, trillion years. You see reader, if I was truly in hell, sex with Kayla would never happen, at least not by choice. I mean, I was seeing the futility of our sin. And it was repulsive. It was hideous. And so was she. And so was I. Our immorality had been a trick. I was duped. I had taken a dollar from a man to buy some candy that gave me false satisfaction and passed up the billion dollars from God, which provided a healthy hearty meal. I knew it. I wanted nothing to do with anything concerning that candy; free or not. What it had cost me is what I would be spending eternity hating and regretting.

I still needed answers, so I asked Miss Kayla if we could sleep. Again she gave the same answer, "Terry, we are in hell." But I was tired, so I climbed into the back seat of the car and tried to sleep. But I soon realized that she wouldn't let me. All she knew was that we should keep driving on this freeway. And it hit me, again. Kayla was compelled to help torment me, and I was probably tormenting her too. I could never rest around her. She would constantly be a dripping faucet in my ear. I told her to please let me sleep. She yelled a high-pitched screech, "Nooooo! We must keep driving on this freeway! Forever!" She looked like a scared 10-year-old. I looked into her eyes, and I said aloud, "I get it you're in hell too, and this is your hell; being with me. Being with this guy who won't let you continue with what you think your hell is." I couldn't take it, and I got out of the car and started running along the freeway yelling, "GOD no! Please have mercy! This cannot be true. I couldn't have missed it. I was so close. I was so close!" I heard Kayla screaming at me in the background over the roaring of the cars flying by. She was saying, "Come back! We have to keep driving!" I left her. And as soon as I was out of earshot of Kayla, "he" introduced himself to me.

I hope you're still with me. I trust you still understand that this is an accurate and true account of what happened. And once again, I have to reiterate how important it is for you to believe. Well like I said, I left Kayla. I began to walk. And when I was away from Kayla, he introduced himself to me by asking me, "Where are you going?" I recognized him right away. I knew him. He used to sometimes whisper to me. He used to whisper temptations. But now he didn't whisper, he spoke to me directly and clearly. Ye are of your father the devil, and the lusts of your father ye will do. He was a murderer from the beginning, and abode not in the truth because there is no truth in him. When he speaketh a lie, he speaketh of his own: for he is a liar and the father of it.

John 8:44

I told him I was getting away from Kayla. He told me that I was his and I would be his for all eternity. He then told me what I already knew. But he was cruel and merciless. He ridiculed me as he spoke of what a fool I was and that I had turned my back on GOD. I told him I didn't believe GOD had given up on me. I told him that I couldn't have missed it! I told him that I was so close. He mockingly said, "There are a zillion others that are saying the same thing. They are all saying, 'I was so close! I was so close!' Everyone says that in the end." He told me what I already knew: "Close doesn't count." He said I had died. And I would spend all eternity with him, and I was his. I still was not 100 percent convinced. I tried to think clearly.

I urge you, brothers and sisters, to watch out for those who cause divisions and put obstacles in your way that are contrary to the teaching you have learned. Keep away from them. For such people are not serving our Lord Christ, but their appetites. By smooth talk and flattery, they deceive the minds of naive people.

Romans 16:17-18 NIV

For wicked and deceitful mouths are opened against me, speaking against me with lying tongues. They encircle me with words of hate and attack me without cause. In return for my love, they accuse me, but I give myself to prayer.

Psalm 109:2-4

The coming of the lawless one is by the activity of Satan with all power and false signs and wonders, and with all wicked deception for those who are perishing because they refused to love the truth and so be saved. Therefore God sends them a strong delusion, so that they may believe what is false, so that all may be condemned who did not believe the truth but had pleasure in unrighteousness. But we ought always to give thanks to God for you, brothers beloved by the Lord because God chose you as the first fruits to be saved through sanctification by the Spirit and belief in the truth.

2Thessaloinians 9:-13

See to it that no one takes you captive by philosophy and empty deceit, according to human tradition, according to the elemental spirits of the world, and not according to Christ.

Colossians 2:8

I had to get my bearings. I thought surely I was walking barefoot along the 405 freeway, and the sun had not changed its position. I thought, "Yes, all the drivers in the cars appear to have the same faces, just in different cars." I thought, "Yes, I drove for 45 minutes, and I didn't pass more than three exits." I thought, "Sure, I drove a second time at speeds of 100 miles an hour, and still, I went nowhere." I thought, "Sure, Kayla told me I was in hell. She told me I had died. And she told me I had chosen her over GOD, and that's why I was here." And now this voice was with me, telling me even more vicious and cruel things. But as I said, I was still not buying into it completely.

I knew there was only one way to be truly sure that I had died and gone to hell. I had to see if I could die! I thought if I could die, then he would be a liar. And I had to be quick. I had to formulate my plan and execute it before he knew what I was up to. You see, he had told me that I was his, and though I didn't believe him, I will admit I was more sure that he was right rather than that he wasn't. So I went for it. I ran headfirst barefoot right onto the freeway. I didn't even look. I just ran. And I ran. I ran as fast as I could. I ran hard. I ran as if I were running for my life. You see, I didn't care that I died because if I died, that would mean that he was a liar;

which would mean I was not in hell. I know readers, it seems unfathom-able that I could have this type of thinking. This type of irrational thinking is something I never thought that I could do. I heard so many stories of grown men and women making incredibly stupid decisions. I often won-dered how someone would choose to walk off a 10 or 15-story building and plummet to their death. And why would a person put a loaded gun to their body and pull the trigger? And why would someone walk or run out in front of fast-moving cars and trucks?

Do you understand that my physical life meant nothing!? My eternal soul was in question. I had to see if I lost my soul. I tried to see if I could die. Can you imagine the surprise of the drivers on the freeway when they saw a grown man barefoot running across three lanes of 65 mph traffic? I ran through three fast-moving lanes barefoot. I didn't even look at the cars. I just kept running nonstop straight across the freeway. I didn't zig-zag. I didn't try to avoid any cars. But more importantly, do you understand how distraught I was when I made it to the divider between Northbound and Southbound without a scratch? I was straddling the divider without a scratch. I had made it halfway without a scratch. I was horrified! But I had yet to make it to the other side. I took off! Again I ran. I didn't look. I just ran again through three lanes of 65 mph traffic. I again made it to the other side without a scratch. I fell to my knees. I was cheerless, dejected, and mournful. I had been so close to making it to heaven. I missed it. I couldn't die because I. Was. Dead.

Chapter VII: X: 99.9999% Is Still Not 100

I was out of my mind with dread. I was out of my mind with loathing. I was heartbroken. I was distraught. I was downcast. I was crying and crying. My mind ached. My eyes were puffy and swollen from weeping. And then I noticed that I was gnashing my teeth. I was gnashing my teeth, so firmly I could taste the salty tang of blood in my mouth. And the one Kayla served, he started to speak to me again. He said I was in hell, that's why I didn't die. I was convinced! I said, "I missed it." I now started to feel a resolve. I mean, I only had that one thing left. I still could accept my fate like a man because I knew that I had been given more than enough chances. I reached into my pockets and pulled out my wallet. I looked at my money. I looked at my I.D. I looked at my credit cards. I thought to myself, all these things were so important. I had been acting like a fool. These things are meaningless when compared to the soul I lost. I screamed, "I was so close!" I hurled my wallet and all of its contents up in the air; where they fell, I didn't watch. I didn't care. Also now (after running through 65 to 80 mph traffic without dying), I was 99.99999% sure I had died and gone to hell.

I immediately thought about all the people who were now in heaven. I was relieved for them. I knew that these people were cut off from us in hell. But I still thought of them having a great time partying and feeling good that all that they had read in the Bible was true.

Finally, brethren, whatsoever things are true, whatsoever things are honest, whatsoever things are just, whatsoever things are pure, whatsoever things are lovely, whatsoever things are of good report; if there be any virtue, and if there be any praise, think on these things.

Philippians 4:8

In my Father's house are many mansions: if it were not so, I would have told you. I go to prepare a place for you.

John 14:2

I also, for the first time, was sure that the Bible was true; everything from Genesis to Revelations was completely factual. Only they (the people in heaven) had held on to God's promise, and my faith had wavered in the end. I knew it. And it was true. I did, however, hold on to the thought that maybe when I and Kayla died, we impacted our old church members to, if need be, repent and get closer to God. And hopefully, our deaths possibly helped motivate them to save more souls. I thought about the utter astonishment on some of the members' faces when they found out that Kayla and I had died in a car accident together, smoking weed and being immoral. Wow! Two people who were GOD fearing, then died when they lost faith and left the church body; that was probably life-changing for people. I started to cry, but then I remembered the scriptures. It was too late for tears. I started to pray, then I stopped because I remembered what the Bible said and knew if I was in hell, it was too late for prayers. I knew if God gave compassion to me because of my repentance after I was in hell, he would be a liar. But I know GOD is infallible. I also knew that if GOD granted my prayer request after coming back and finding my back turned against him, the Bible would have to be a lie. But I knew God was not a liar, and the Bible was true. Once again, I just said, "I missed it. I was so close; so very close."

The person Kayla served was still whispering to me. Some of the things he said truly showed he was the king of discouragement; he had the gift of discouragement, and he was using that gift on me. Right now. And then that's when he suggested I cut my private part off (but he used the epithet word). At first, I didn't think that's what he was saying. But he whispered it to me over and over. And then yes, I knew that was really what he wanted me to do. And wouldn't you know, right at my feet was a 6-inch razor-sharp piece of broken mirror. "Scary" is the only word that describes what was going on with me. This voice went on to explain why he wanted me to commit this act. He said that I loved my private part so much in heaven. I asked, "What do you mean I loved it in heaven?" He said, "Down here, we consider where you were, we consider that to be heaven. You see, we don't get to go to (the real) heaven, but we get to go to earth, and since that's the best we got, that's our heaven. And you just gave up real heaven." He said, "You loved your 'epithet word' in heaven, well we love them down here in hell. And we're going to have a lot of fun with it. He said that my epithet was going to get touched a lot down here. He said, "Don't even ever think about Kayla again. She won't be touching you. She's gone back for others." (I couldn't find her anywhere. But I didn't expect to. I was in hell, and hell is lonely. Hell is a place without hope. Period.) He was cruel. So mean. But he was so right. And that made it worse. I picked up the 6-inch, razor-sharp, broken piece of mirror. I turned and looked at the side of the mirror with the reflection. I saw myself. I saw myself lonely and in hell. He said, "You might as well cut it off before we get to it." He said, "What does it matter now? You won't need it here. And it will be better for you if you cut it off before we get to it." He was making sense. He said, "Remember how you just ran across six lanes of fast-moving traffic while not looking and barefoot? You didn't die. You can't die! You are in hell. You are mine! We will have fun with it. Cut it off!" I felt controlled. I turned the sharp edge toward me. I thought, "What's the difference? I missed it. I let God down. I'm in hell for eternity. No more kids. No more family. No more desires. I'm standing on the side of the freeway. Nobody cares. I'm in hell. The sun is so high in the sky. The mountains look so dreary. The cars just keep making that terrible zooming-by sound. The air is dry and still. I'm all alone." I pulled down my pants and got in a position to do what he told me I should do. I stayed there in that position, just thinking. I was just distraught. I was sad. But still, I said, "No! I said, "I don't care that you have to do your job. I'm not going to help. I don't care. I missed it. I'm a loser." I threw the glass down. I pulled up my britches and just kept walking. I just walked. And I walked; forever and ever. I was in hell.

Chapter VIII: The Sweetness of False Hope

He said, "But we will start the pain soon." He was patient. He told me that I was a fool. He said he sent Kayla to tempt me. He said she was just a vessel, and I chose her instead of GOD. He told me everything was ripe for him to steal my soul from GOD when I died. I could only listen. He went on and spoke about all the people who tried to get me to repent and get closer to the Church body. He said, "You wouldn't even listen to Dave Kim" (Kim is the lead evangelist at my church). He said, "That man did so much work for God. He spat, "That man loved you, and you turned your back on all of his words because you were too prideful to believe." I knew it was all true. He told me that whenever I'm about to see my children, he attacks me because I'm not alert at that time. He said Kayla died years ago, and she serves him, and soon I would be sent back to do his dominion too. I continued to walk, simply sad. I continued to walk, simply distraught. I continued to walk, simply downcast. I continued to walk, just thinking about Jesus. And I continued to walk and think of what I had given up. I continued to walk and drag my feet. My feet were starting to bleed, crack and hurt. I had a tank top on. I had sweatsuit bottoms on. I was filthy. I had been rolling around on the ground crying. I had been rolling in the dirt because I was in hell. In hell, what else do you have but dirt? I was starting to embrace it. I had missed the glorious coming of Jesus Christ. I had missed it! I was screaming at the top of my lungs. I was screaming in my head. Over and over, I was screaming, "I'm sorry! I missed it! I missed it! I missed it! Why? Why? Why?!" He continued to talk to me. I continued to listen. He was telling me that there are rules even in hell. I listened and walked. He told me it was all lost. He said it was hopeless. I knew it was, too. I watched the cars zoom by me; the same old faces driving a lot of different cars; the same sun in the sky. I was so thirsty. I watched the cars. And I suddenly saw something different. I saw something I hadn't seen before since I had gotten to hell. I saw a fire truck. It was moving slowly, and it was on the freeway. I was surprised to see the scenery change, but I know that he is very powerful in hell, and he can make hell any way he wants. Here, he is the boss. I watched the fire truck. It came toward me. He explained that the fire truck was his and they were going to come and get me and take me to where the new arrivals to hell go. I believed him. I knew the torture was about to start. I was in hell. The fire truck pulled up to me. Three men jumped out of the fire truck. They surrounded me. They asked me what I was doing walking around the freeway. They asked other seemingly dumb questions like, what was I doing? Who was I? What happened? Where was I going? And was I drinking or using drugs? And where were my shoes? And where was my car? And why didn't I use the emergency phone? All questions that his demons already knew the answers to. If I wasn't in hell, I would have laughed at the fact they were pretending that they weren't working for him and picking me up to start torturing me. Then one of them asked me if I needed a ride to the nearest gas station. I played along and said ok. I got in their truck. I heard one of the officers over the two-way radio say that they needed another pickup as soon as possible. I saw all three guys look at each other, and I knew they were taking me further into hell. I was thoroughly sure. I mean, I was scared, but as I said earlier, I was resolved. I knew my sinfulness. I knew the chances I had been given. And I had missed the return of our savior. When Jesus came back, I was not ready. And I had missed the chance for salvation. I had turned my back on Jesus and the cross. So I rode in silence with demons. I expected any minute for them to stop messing with my mind and start all the horrors that were due for people like me who rejected the son of GOD. After exiting the freeway, they asked me if I wanted to get dropped off at the gas station. I said, "Yes," still not believing that they were who they said they were. We reached the gas station two minutes later. They parked. The door was opened. I got out. I slowly walked away. I first turned right. I then turned left. I walked for a while. I was scared to have hope. I couldn't allow him to have fun with me by making me believe I wasn't in hell. I knew the scriptures. You don't leave hell. You never leave hell. It is forever, weeping and gnashing of teeth. There I stood, dirty and thirty... I was barefoot with cracked and sore feet. I had no Identification. I had no money, except four pennies in my sweatsuit pants pocket. I had missed it. I was in the place we go, for those who miss it. I was hopeless. I walked into a fast-food restaurant. I thought that he was so cruel. He played such cruel tricks. Hell was so wrong. Hell had only one rule: there are no rules of hell. It is steadily evolving – if you will? I was being tormented with false hope. This is truly the only thing that can hurt someone in hell. I asked for water in the restaurant. The woman behind the counter gave me a 'you are disgusting look' and then reluctantly gave me a small courtesy cup. I thought ok, the cup is about to disappear any minute. The faucet would only yield sand, or worse, he would give me water so I could establish false hope. This was my hell. Readers, are you there? I want you to understand that I believed I was in hell. I believed I had died.

The faucet turned out to yield water. I drank it. It was wet, and it was cold. I walked outside. I was barefoot, and my feet were so damaged I had a hobble. I had no money. I asked passersby for money. I told them I was stranded and needed to make a phone call. I finally got 50 cents after asking about 10 people. They all thought I wanted to buy drugs or alcohol. I looked very bad. I went to a payphone, but I remembered my phone was gone. And it contained all of my phone numbers. I only knew two numbers by heart. I called the first: my friend and brother in Christ, Deon Gordon. I called the second: My mother.

A LETTER TO THE READER:

Luke 13:22-30, Then Jesus went through the towns and villages, teaching as he made his way to Jerusalem. Someone asked him, Lord, are only a few people going to be saved? '' He said to them, "Make every effort to enter through the narrow door because many, I tell you, will try to enter and will not be able to. Once the owner of the house gets up and closes the door, you will stand outside knocking and pleading for 'sir, open the door for us.' But He will answer, 'I don't know you or where you come from. Then you will say, 'We ate and drank with you, and you taught in our streets. But He will reply," I don't know you or where you come from. Away from me, all you evildoers! There will be weeping there and gnashing of teeth when you see Abraham, Isaac, and Jacob and all the prophets of the Kingdom of God, but you yourselves thrown out.

I want to first thank you for reading this account. This account lasted between three and five hours. I'm not exactly sure. I am sure that this is a true account. I have spoken with Kayla. She is fine; physically. She can verify most of the story, but we all know there are three sides to every story, hers, mine, and God's. She still is unsure if she is alive. As of today, I feel the same way. But I have come to confess my sins. I've prayed. I've reconnected with Jesus. I'm not saying I'm not going to sin. I'm not Jesus; meaning I'm not without sin. But I don't want to be arrogant in my sin. Also, sin played a role. Guilt played a role. And Kayla (in my opinion), opened herself up to be used as a vessel. When she was in that so-called seizure, I believe she was possessed; possessed by a spirit with the convincing and comforting nature of the character of Morpheus, played by Laurence Fishburn, in the movie The Matrix. I believe someone had died on that patch of the freeway, and that spirit had attacked Kayla and me based on all of the elements being the way they were (drugs, sins, guilt, etc.). This made it perfect to try and trick us and steal our souls. But that's my opinion. And now that you have heard the whole story, you can formulate your own opinion.

 And thirdly and lastly, yes it is true, I did not go to hell. No one goes to hell and leaves. I don't even want you to necessarily believe in hell as a place you or I could go. Whatever hell is, it was not created for you or me. Matthew 25:41 Then he will say to those on his left, 'Depart from me you who are cursed, into the eternal fire prepared for the devil and his angels.' The biggest point I want you to understand is that God disciplines those he loves. Hebrews 12:6 Because the Lord disciplines the one he loves, and he chastens everyone he accepts as his son." God stepped in to get me to take notice of the unrighteous way I was living. And He stepped in to get me to repent.

But one thing I must ask of you reader (like I said I would in the story) is that you believe; that you believe these things happened. I don't want you to believe I went to hell. But I want you to believe that I believed I went to hell. I have to believe I didn't miss it. I have to believe that I am still GOD's child. And God has not abandoned me because of my sin. I plan to do anything I have to do to make sure I stay connected to the body; and if not this church, then anyone that I could stay in "fellowship." But one thing I know will help me come to terms with whether I'm alive is if I can do GOD's work still. I believe no one in hell or no one dead can help save souls for Jesus. And if just one person because of this piece is changed or saved or both, I must be alive, and I must still have a chance for salvation. Please send me an email with your comments, concerns, criticisms, advice, or helpful hints. Please also email me any accounts you have had similar to the one I had. Also, tell me if this has helped to strengthen your faith or save you! You may email me at giveinfo@syb1.org. Share with me similar stories that you have had. I know they're out there. I know he's not just attacking me. Let's get our testimonies out. All of your testimonies, stories, and your emails will be included in part 2, book two: "The Day I Went to Hell: Kayla's Side."

For as he thinketh in his heart, so is he: Eat and drink, saith he to thee; but his heart is not with thee.

Proverbs 23:7

Where there is no vision, the people perish: but he that keepeth the law, happy is he.

Proverbs 29:18

We have to do what we can to help save each other. Remember, the enemy wants to separate you from those who support and love you. Stay in the safety of GOD and His people, and you will be protected. Please pray for me right after the completion of your reading of this account. And now I have prayed for you. It's done.

God bless you.

Experienced and Written by

T.L.Grundy

God Disciplines His Sons

For the Lord disciplines the one he loves, and he chastises every son He receives." Endure suffering as discipline; God is treating you as sons. For what son is not disciplined by his father? If you do not experience discipline like everyone else, then you are illegitimate children and not a true son.

Hebrews 12:6-8

Berean Study Bible

Media&SoulProductions

www.ingramcontent.com/pod-product-compliance
Lightning Source LLC
Chambersburg PA
CBHW040858070726
47599CB00035B/2043